C000063009

HOW TO BE BRAVE

by Siân Owen

samuelfrench.co.uk

Copyright © 2019 by Siân Owen
All Rights Reserved

HOW TO BE BRAVE is fully protected under the copyright laws of the British Commonwealth, including Canada, the United States of America, and all other countries of the Copyright Union. All rights, including professional and amateur stage productions, recitation, lecturing, public reading, motion picture, radio broadcasting, television and the rights of translation into foreign languages are strictly reserved.

ISBN 978-0-573-11676-6

www.samuelfrench.co.uk
www.samuelfrench.com

FOR AMATEUR PRODUCTION ENQUIRIES

UNITED KINGDOM AND WORLD
EXCLUDING NORTH AMERICA
plays@samuelfrench.co.uk
020 7255 4302/01

Each title is subject to availability from Samuel French,
depending upon country of performance.

CAUTION: Professional and amateur producers are hereby warned that *HOW TO BE BRAVE* is subject to a licensing fee. Publication of this play does not imply availability for performance. Both amateurs and professionals considering a production are strongly advised to apply to the appropriate agent before starting rehearsals, advertising, or booking a theatre. A licensing fee must be paid whether the title is presented for charity or gain and whether or not admission is charged.

The professional rights in this play are controlled by The Agency (London) Ltd, 24 Pottery Ln, Notting Hill, London W11 4LZ.

No one shall make any changes in this title for the purpose of production. No part of this book may be reproduced, stored in a retrieval system, or transmitted in any form, by any means, now known or yet to be invented, including mechanical, electronic, photocopying, recording, videotaping, or otherwise, without the prior written permission of the publisher. No one shall upload this title, or part of this title, to any social media websites.

The right of Siân Owen to be identified as author of this work has been asserted in accordance with Section 77 of the Copyright, Designs and Patents Act 1988.

THINKING ABOUT PERFORMING A SHOW?

There are thousands of plays and musicals available to perform from Samuel French right now, and applying for a licence is easier and more affordable than you might think

From classic plays to brand new musicals, from monologues to epic dramas, there are shows for everyone.

Plays and musicals are protected by copyright law, so if you want to perform them, the first thing you'll need is a licence. This simple process helps support the playwright by ensuring they get paid for their work and means that you'll have the documents you need to stage the show in public.

Not all our shows are available to perform all the time, so it's important to check and apply for a licence before you start rehearsals or commit to doing the show.

LEARN MORE & FIND THOUSANDS OF SHOWS

Browse our full range of plays and musicals, and find out more about how to license a show

www.samuelfrench.co.uk/perform

Talk to the friendly experts in our Licensing team for advice on choosing a show and help with licensing

plays@samuelfrench.co.uk   020 7387 9373

Acting Editions

BORN TO PERFORM

Playscripts designed from the ground up to work the way you do in rehearsal, performance and study

---

Larger, clearer text for easier reading

Wider margins for notes

Performance features such as character and props lists, sound and lighting cues, and more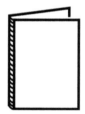

+ CHOOSE A SIZE AND STYLE TO SUIT YOU

STANDARD EDITION

Our regular paperback book at our regular size

SPIRAL-BOUND EDITION

The same size as the Standard Edition, but with a sturdy, easy-to-fold, easy-to-hold spiral-bound spine

LARGE EDITION

A4 size and spiral bound, with larger text and a blank page for notes opposite every page of text – perfect for technical and directing use

---

LEARN MORE | **samuelfrench.co.uk/actingeditions**

MUSIC USE NOTE

Licensees are solely responsible for obtaining formal written permission from copyright owners to use copyrighted music in the performance of this play and are strongly cautioned to do so. If no such permission is obtained by the licensee, then the licensee must use only original music that the licensee owns and controls. Licensees are solely responsible and liable for all music clearances and shall indemnify the copyright owners of the play(s) and their licensing agent, Samuel French, against any costs, expenses, losses and liabilities arising from the use of music by licensees. Please contact the appropriate music licensing authority in your territory for the rights to any incidental music.

USE OF COPYRIGHT MUSIC

A licence issued by Samuel French Ltd to perform this play does not include permission to use the incidental music specified in this copy.

Where the place of performance is already licensed by the PERFORMING RIGHT SOCIETY (PRS) a return of the music used must be made to them. If the place of performance is not so licensed then application should be made to the PRS, 2 Pancras Square, London, N1C 4AG. www.prsformusic.com

A separate and additional licence from PHONOGRAPHIC PERFORMANCE LTD, 1 Upper James Street, London W1F 9DE (www.ppluk.com) is needed whenever commercial recordings are used.

IMPORTANT BILLING AND CREDIT REQUIREMENTS

If you have obtained performance rights to this title, please refer to your licensing agreement for important billing and credit requirements.

AUTHOR'S NOTE

Around the time I was asked to write a play for Dirty Protest, I needed to find some brave.
I had loads when I was a little girl. But I seemed to have lost it along the way.
And I needed it back.
So I started looking back.
I dug deep.
Into what has come before and this lead me to think about what I would leave behind. To do this I had to really explore what I am made of. In spirit and personality, but also what am I actually made of – what are the particles in me, what is in my blood, what I have breathed in? And I found out that we are made of star dust and my hands got tingles and I knew that I had to pour all of this into the melting pot of this play. But also I wanted to look at where I was made. This play is set in Newport, South Wales. Where I was born and bred. I hate how Newport is so often maligned – looked down on. It is actually a city full of courage and tenacity and history and I wanted to explore and explode this spirit. And in doing so I celebrated the well-known stories but also uncovered unheard voices and tales, and I understood the importance of what they could teach us.
So what should I call this play full of all this magic and what we are made of? I almost called it *How To Be Brave?* But after I uncovered all I had, the title couldn't be a question. It had to be a statement of who we are and what we have done. It had to be *How To Be Brave.* To celebrate the bravery in the everyday and all the days that have come before.

How To Be Brave is a one-woman play told through the eyes of Katie, a mother determined that her young daughter will never lose the powerful, fierce magic she arrived into the world with.

This play can be performed both in the round and end on.

Siân Owen, July 2019

How To Be Brave, produced by Dirty Protest Theatre with Chapter and Newport Library, Museum and Art Gallery, was first performed at Chapter, Cardiff on 13 March 2019.

It toured:

Chapter, Cardiff	13–16 March
Torch Theatre, Milford Haven	19 March
Le Pub, Newport	21–23 March
Galeri, Caernarfon	27 March
Community House, Newport	29 March
Machynlleth Comedy Festival	4 May
Wasing Woodlands	4 & 11 July
Roundabout @ Summerhall, Edinburgh Festival Fringe	
	31 July – 25 August
Theatr Clwyd	3–4 September
Aberystwyth Arts Centre	6 September
Llanelli Ffwrnes	7 September

CAST & CREATIVES

Performer	Laura Dalgleish
Writer	Siân Owen
Director	Catherine Paskell
Producer	Shane Nickels
Designer	Cory Shipp
Lighting Designer	Dave Beever
Sound Designer	Dan Lawrence
Choreographer	Bridie Smith
Engagement Coordinator	Naz Syed
Engagement Assistant	Angela Harris
Marketing Manager	Rhian Lewis
Production Manager	Dave Beever
Cover illustration by	Nic Finch @ Chameleonic

Dirty Protest Theatre are: Matthew Bulgo, Branwen Davies, Angela Harris, Catherine Paskell & Tim Price

Supported by Arts Council of Wales, Welsh Government and Lottery funding

CAST & CREATIVES

LAURA DALGLEISH – PERFORMER

Performer Laura Dalgleish's screen credits include: the BBC multi-platform comedy *Halfway*, as well as *Ordinary Lies* (Series 2); *Call the Midwife* and *Eastenders*. On stage, Laura's credits include: *Much Ado About Nothing, The Tempest, Swallows and Amazons* (Storyhouse Theatre, Chester – 2018 Rep Company), *Horrible Christmas* (Lowry and Alexandra Palace), three No.1 tours of *Horrible Histories*, and *Heart Shaped Hole* (PLAYlist Festival for Theatre 503). Laura is also a skilled voiceover artist, voicing characters for *Torchwood* audio dramas *The Hope* and *Aliens Among Us*, as well as the Big Finish Original Production *Blind Terror:The Gods of Frost*. Laura also stars in the BBC Radio Wales comedy series *Bravo Two Charlies*.

SIÂN OWEN – WRITER

Writer Siân Owen was born and brought up in Newport. She is a graduate of the MA Writing for Performance programme at Goldsmiths College. Siân has written for Pentabus, *This Land*, and for BBC Radio 4, *Pieces*. Her play *Restoration* won the Oxford Playhouse New Writing Competition. Siân is currently under commission with Box of Tricks Theatre Company, and has been part of the Sherman Cymru Advanced Writers Group, and the Royal Court Studio Group.

CATHERINE PASKELL – DIRECTOR

Director Catherine Paskell is Artistic Director of Dirty Protest Theatre and an independent performance director from Cardiff. Previous to this she was a founding Creative Associate of National Theatre Wales. She is a Fellow of the Clore Leadership Programme and the RSA, and an Arts Associate for the Arts Council of Wales.
Catherine's recent directing credits for Dirty Protest Theatre include: *Sugar Baby* by Alan Harris, which returned to ROUNDABOUT at the Edinburgh Fringe in 2018 after an acclaimed run in 2017, when it was added to the British Council Showcase as one of the best new shows that year. By public demand, *Sugar Baby* toured Wales, then Germany and transferred to the Soho Theatre. Last year, Catherine directed a new family play celebrating the link between Wales' shipbuilding

industry and Star Wars, *Lightspeed to Pembroke Dock* by Mark Williams which toured fourteen venues in Wales. Her touring production of *Parallel Lines* by Katherine Chandler won Best Production in the English Language at the Theatre Critics of Wales Awards. Recent independent directing includes: a new translation of *The Merchant of Venice* written in Portuguese by playwright Marcos Barbosa and staged in Brazil, and new play *Twisted Tales* for Institute of the Arts Barcelona. Catherine has also directed productions for companies including Sherman Theatre, Wales Millennium Centre, The Junket Club, Unity Theatre Liverpool, Theatre 503, Oldham Coliseum, Tara Arts, Soho Theatre, and Lyric Theatre Hammersmith.

She is a founding Creative Associate of National Theatre Wales. Between 2009-2011, she helped start the organisation from scratch, building it from four people working in coffee shops to a £2-million core-funded national arts institution. She directed the fifth production in the inaugural season, *The Beach*, an interactive play with digital storytelling performed on the Prestatyn seafront. She created the landmark New Critics programme, working with national arts journalists to develop cultural criticism in Wales, and she directed The Assembly "debate and respond" cultural democracy programme which she continues to deliver for NTW (now known as "Performance Parties") where local writers, artists and audiences debate and respond creatively to local issues.

Catherine trained on the Theatre Directing MFA at Birkbeck, University of London and was resident director at Contact, Manchester and Octagon Theatre Bolton.

SHANE NICKELS – PRODUCER

Shane is a creative producer working across theatre, live games and experiences. Shane has a passion for the creative process, challenging the accepted norm and creating opportunities that ensure the arts are for everybody. Shane thrives in projects with a powerful voice and innovative vision and collaborating with artists and organisations who enjoy doing things differently. Collaborations with: yello brick, Dirty Protest, August012, National Theatre Wales, Fio, The Other Room, Wales Millennium Centre, Machynlleth Comedy Festival, Greenman Festival, Welsh National Opera, Cardiff University, University of Wales Trinity Saint David. Shane is a freelance lecturer at UWTSD and was also 1st AD on BAFTA Cymru winning *Dancing In Circles*.

CORY SHIPP – DESIGNER

Cory trained at the Royal Welsh College of Music and Drama after working for six years as a Scenic Artist. She now works all across the UK as a Set and Costume Designer for theatre, musicals and other ranges of performative work. Previous work includes: *How to Be Brave* (Dirty Protest); *Company* (University of South Wales, Trinity St. David); *The Mikvah Project, Pilgrims, 8GB of Hardcore Pornography* and *Sadness and Joy in the Life of Giraffes* (Orange Tree Theatre, Richmond); *Pippin* (University of South Wales, Trinity St. David); *Easy Virtue* (The Watermill Theatre, Newbury); *Word Gets Around* (Rhondda Cynon Taff Theatres) and most recently, *Unfortunate The Musical* (Costume Designer/Fat Rascal Theatre Company).

DAVE BEEVER – LIGHTING DESIGNER / PRODUCTION MANAGER

Dave studied Lighting Design & Production Management at Northbrook College, Sussex graduating in 2007 with a Foundation Degree.

Freelance work has included: Birmingham International Dance Festival, Dirty Protest, Courtyard Hereford and too many years of Edinburgh Fringe to remember.

Dave is currently Production Manager at Zoo Venues for Edinburgh Festival Fringe, Production Manager for 2faced Dance and is proud to be involved with Dirty Protest and *How To Be Brave* as Lighting Designer and Production Manager.

DAN LAWRENCE – SOUND DESIGNER

Dan was raised in Aberystwyth and went on to study Pop Music and Recording in Salford, graduating in 1992. He has lived in Cardiff since 2003 and has worked as a composer, musical director and sound designer with many Welsh theatre companies including: Dirty Protest (*Sugar Baby, Lightspeed From Pembroke Dock, Parallel Lines*); National Theatre Wales (*A Good Night Out in the Valleys, De Gabay, Mother Courage*); Theatr Genedlaethol Cymru (*Y Storm, Y Negesydd, Y Fenyw Ddaeth o'r Môr*); Sherman Cymru (*Ho Ho Ho, Pinocchio, The Elves & the Shoemakers, The Princess & the Pea, The Emperor's New Clothes*); Theatr Iolo; Taking Flight Theatre; Hijinx; Gagglebabble and West Yorkshire Playhouse.

Dan also runs his own recording studio in Cardiff, tutors young bands and continues to perform regularly with the traditional Welsh folk duo Olion Byw, and the Welsh / Galician collaboration band Maelog.

BRIDIE SMITH – CHOREOGRAPHER

Bridie has been a choreographer for over ten years with most projects being based in theatre plays and musicals. From day to day she runs a successful performance academy across Pontypridd in South Wales which offers dance, drama, acro and cheer classes. Bridie is also an actress who trained at the Royal Welsh College of Music and Drama.

Choreographing *How To Brave* was an absolute joy and the feedback has been so humbling. Bridie can't wait to see it continue its tour at Edinburgh Fringe and hopes many of the audience will find nostalgic childhood memories in the dancing.

NAZ SYED – ENGAGEMENT COORDINATOR

Naz is a Welsh-Persian freelance visual artist, designer and teacher. With twenty years of experience working in community and education settings across a range of visual art disciplines, specialising in costume, textiles, mixed media and applied arts. She also works in different creative aspects as a community engagement officer and events manager. Naz is an Arts Award adviser, facilitator for the Night Out Project for Arts Council of Wales and Fusion Coordinator in Newport. Naz worked on *How to be Brave* as our Newport ambassador! Focusing on community engagement and a Night Out Project facilitator.

"I am passionate about supporting the arts and its power to connect communities and empower people. Bringing arts to the heart of the community and for the arts to be inclusive and accessible to all. I love hearing people's stories and seeing them grow. I have experienced how being involved in a creative project can inspire change, confidence and belonging in people. It was wonderful to be a part of *How To Be Brave*, an inspiring story that embraces Newport, my home town."

She has collaborated with: Walk The Plank, Circo Rum Ba Ba, Puppet Soup, Odd Doll, Kid Carpet, Untied Artists, Fio, Dirty Protest theatre, Tin Shed Theatre, Half a String, Circus Berzercus.

ASHA OSBORNE-GRINTER – STAGE MANAGER
(EDINBURGH FRINGE 2019)

Previous work includes: *I Caught Crabs in Walberswick* (PRSC); *Elise* (Edinburgh Fringe Festival 2018, Pleasance Courtyard); *Smalltown Boy* (The Island); *Posh* (Alma Tavern); *Hot Flush* (Edinburgh Fringe Festival 2019, Gilded Balloon).

She is currently an artist-in-residence at The Island, Bristol and the Artistic Director of Dixie Fried Theatre.

JOSH BOWLES – STAGE MANAGER (AUTUMN 2019)

Initially taking to theatre as a musician, Josh transitioned into stage management and sound design, combining his engineering and technical experience to bring organisational and creative deftness to various theatrical productions.

Recent stage management credits include: *Lovecraft (Not The Sex Shop in Cardiff)* (Carys Eleri / Wales Millennium Centre); *Louder Is Not Always Clearer* (Mr & Mrs Clark); *Meet Fred* (Hijinx Theatre / Blind Summit); *Cardiff Boy* (Red Oak Theatre / The Other Room); *The Flop* (Hijinx Theatre / Spymonkey); *Camp Be Yourself* (Box. Theatre); *Dames* (Siberian Lights) and Sound Operator on *Alice In Wonderland* (Sherman Theatre).

Dirty Protest Theatre
Wales' National New Writing Company.

Launched in 2007, the company has produced over 300 new plays by over 300 established and emerging writers, including Welsh writers: Katherine Chandler, Gary Owen, Brad Birch, Alan Harris, Daf James, Ed Thomas, Kelly Jones, Tim Price, and Meredydd Barker; and British playwrights including: Duncan Macmillan, Rebecca Lenkiewicz, James Graham, Joel Horwood, Chloe Moss, Lucy Kirkwood, and Jack Thorne.

Dirty Protest Theatre have created performances with partners including Theatr Clwyd; Paines Plough; Almeida Theatre; the Royal Court Theatre; Soho Theatre; Traverse Theatre, Edinburgh; Camden Roundhouse; National Theatre Wales; Chapter, Cardiff; Galeri, Caernarfon; Aberystwyth Arts Centre; Newport Riverfront; The Torch, Milford Haven; and Sherman Theatre, Cardiff.

Dirty Protest stage original contemporary plays in theatres and alternative venues, including pubs and clubs, music festivals, kebab shops, hairdressers and forests. Alongside full-length productions, Dirty Protest stage regular short play nights where established and emerging writers are presented on the same platform, providing opportunities for writers, directors and actors. These nights present a shot of theatrical tequila without the paraphernalia, all for the price of a pint.

Twitter: @DirtyProtest
Instagram: @dirtyprotesttheatre
Facebook: @dirtyprotesttheatre
Website: Dirtyprotesttheatre.co.uk

ACKNOWLEDGEMENTS

My utmost thanks to the following people, without whom we could not have made *How To Be Brave*: Dave Beever; Claire Broome; Josh Dugdale; Gwyn Emberton; Nic Finch; Rebecca Gould; Jackson Green; Angela Harris; Dan Lawrence; Rhian Lewis; Jennifer Lunn; Kirsten McTernan; Danny Muir; Emma Newrick; Shane Nickels; Eilir Owen-Griffiths; Benjamin Partridge; Luca Patricolo; Alex Priestley; Nick Quinn; Bridie Smith; Naz Syed; Cory Shipp; Peter Strong; Jamie Waugh; Barbara Bartl, John Brodrick, Alun Prescott and everyone at Newport Central Library, Museum and Art Gallery; Sam Dabb and all at Le Pub; Rob Jones and all in The Murenger; Michael Parry and Heather Edwards from the Newport Resilient Communities Central Team; Peter and Mary from Newport Photos; Charlie, Steven and all at Samuel French; British Council Wales; Fortnum & Mason; National Theatre Wales; Paines Plough; Theatr Clwyd; University of Wales Trinity Saint David; Wales Millennium Centre, and everyone at Wasing Estate.

A very special thank you to Frank and Elizabeth Brenan for their kindness and generosity.

Our thanks to everyone who has donated their time and money to the production.

Dirty Protest are Matthew Bulgo, Branwen Davies, Angela Harris, Catherine Paskell and Tim Price and they are a special kind of magic. Thank you all for your belief and faith and your help in developing this play.

A very special thank you to Catherine Paskell for her belief, support, guidance, her time, her passion and talent. And for her constant encouragement.

A massive thank you to Laura Dagleish whose extraordinary talent shone through this whole process.

My eternal thanks to my family and friends for their endless everything. My amazing Mum and Dad and my legend of a husband, Dan. And to Z and E, you teach me what being brave means every day.

And thank you to Newport. I hope I've done you proud.

This play is dedicated to all the women of Newport.
Now and then.
Especially my Mum and my Grandma.

I usually can't say things out loud. I am a librarian after all.

I bloody love books. When I was a kid, my Nan gave me loads of books. Books on cars, stars, bakes, how-to-makes. I have them all in Dewey Decimal Order. Like I do at the library. So I know where everything should be.

I'm so organised. I even assign different ring tones on my phone. Work: Wuthering Heights, Kate Bush. The Hospital: Staying Alive, The Bee Gees. My Mother: theme tune to Jaws. I love an order. A routine.

I should be at work today. It's a Wednesday. I work in the Central Library in John Frost Square. Named after the famous Chartist John Frost. Now they've built a new shopping centre there called Friar's Walk named after I assume, some monk, Friar Fuck Knows.

But I need to be here today.

Because today is the day.

Today is marked on the calendar with stars all around it and a big red circle. It's planned down to the minute.

I come downstairs and see my Little One. Sometimes I just have to stop. And gaze at her. At her light. I don't understand how the universe gave her to me. It blows my mind. All of it. How much I love her. I made her.

And she's all golden hair and sleepy and oh, absolutely covered in my make-up.

My new lipstick is all over her nose. And ears.

(Beat.)

Mum's in the kitchen. But I don't go in there. Because if we are in the same room as each other for more than about two minutes, one of us'll get fifteen for murder. Life, if I really get stuck in.

I've made a rota but Mum's not bloody sticking to it. She's making the breakfast but that's my job. She's supposed to be doing the washing. I don't understand her washing machine. It's got too many dials. Mine's all buttons. I miss mine already. I miss my house. I miss having the heating off. And Netflix. Little One misses Netflix too. And Alexa. Mum won't let us install Alexa. *I don't trust her,* she says. *Her or her voice.* She doesn't even keep her ketchup in the fridge.

We won't be here long. We are just here for a bit you know, just for the extra pair of hands. Little One's dad is not in the picture. Thank God. And here we are, with Mum, in the house I grew up in, with the same curfews and rules. And everything feels cramped and everything is on top of me and I'm supposed to make a nice breakfast but Mum is in the bloody kitchen doing it.

So I go into the living room, and Little One is trying to fold up her rainbow wings, the ones she wears everywhere. Only they keep popping open so she has to lie on them.

And she picks up these massive scissors, the ones Mum makes her dancing costumes with.

And she gathers all her superhero costumes and Elsa cape, cuts them up, and puts them into a bin bag.

I try and grab the scissors and I step on a piece of Lego. *JESUS! Where are my fucking shoes?*

And Little One says, *Tommy Norris said girls can't be superheroes and can't wear capes, they're not strong and brave.*

What? Does Tommy Norris' mother know his views on this? Because I think she would be very interested to hear what he thinks.

Tommy Snotty Norris.

They can afford all the clobber but not tissues apparently.

What did you say?

SHUT UP SNOTBAGS.

Now that's not a very nice thing to say is it? Why'd you say that to him for?

I was cross, and then I got sad. Because I'm not strong enough am I? And I need to be really brave today. Don't I, Mummy?

And I don't know what to say.

(Beat.)

And Mum runs in, *Why have you given her those scissors?*

Me? This is your fault.

I didn't give them to her Katie.

And Little One proudly announces: *I got them myself! I climbed up on the big dresser.*

And Mum shrieks, *Katie, you need to be with her, you should be watching her like a hawk.*

But this is your house, Mum!

And you're her mother, so start acting like it please.

Mum's toast starts burning and the smoke alarm goes off. And Mum shrieks, *WHAT IS IT WITH YOU KATIE?* And I am all like, *Mum, TURN THE ALARM OFF*, and Little One is *Uh oh.*

And I go to open the window but the windows are locked and we're coughing and it stinks of burning toast and I'm boiling. It's like the tropics in Mum's house. And Little One is pulling on my arm.

Mum, Mum, Mum, Mummy, Mummy, MUMMY, I NEEEEDDDDDDD YOU.

WHAT?

I see Little One and she's holding up her hand and she's cut her finger on the bastard scissors and there's blood.

I'm not good with blood. I faint when my body feels any kind of pain at all. Giving birth was a fucking nightmare.

Little One looks at me and says, *what if today goes wrong all like this?*

And Mum runs to Little One with some Avengers plasters and I yell at them, *I CAN'T STAND THIS!*

I open the front door to get some air and the smoke pours out down the road and for some reason, I don't know why, I just follow it.

I run to the Londis and Mum's neighbour, Mo, is coming out with some milk. And she says, *You OK love? Why are you crying?* And I take the milk out of her hand and gulp it down because there's smoke and choke in my throat. I run down to the Civic Centre. I'm sick in a bin.

I sprint down Bridge Street. I almost get knocked over by The Queen's Hotel.

And I'm hairing down the high street and the rapper guy is rapping GANGSTA'S PARADISE into a microphone and it's really fucking loud so as I run past, I turn the speaker off and now rapper guy is chasing me and I turn into Friar's Walk, John Frost Square, Friar's Walk. And he's still after me so I jump into somebody's tent that they have put up for the night. And I just sit there. In an empty tent. I feel awful. What am I doing? I don't know, I don't know what's wrong with me but I can't stay here. So I get out.

Then it starts to piss down.

I don't even have a coat on me. All I have is the emergency wet wipes in my pocket and £5.34 in change. That's got to last me until next week.

I need to get out the fucking rain and the library is in front of me.

(Beat.)

I'm by the information desk.

Why are you here today?

And there's Derek.

Now I have a proper soft spot for Derek. He is my Mum's friend. Her dance partner. And he's super kind. He picks her up and takes her to their ballroom dance classes on Queen's Hill. A real gent. I don't know why he likes my mother. He's always visiting the library. He reads the papers. I like him so much but today for some reason I say, *I'm going to have a disco Derek! A fucking roller disco.* I mean, what-the-fuck?!

And he says, *You look a bit flustered love,* and starts to hang about, watching me. With his kind eyes.

I hide in the self-help section.

I hide in the health section.

Then I hide in the science section and there's Derek again and he whispers, *Seeing as you're here, can I have a bit of help? I need to pay my gas bill on the interweb.*

NOT NOW DEREK.

And he's so kind, I don't know why I'm being so mean to him. Watching him hobble off I think I'm going to cry.

Then I go up the spiral stairs to the Local History section because I know Derek can't follow me up there with his dicky knee.

And I see a book, "Notable People from Newport".

And I've never seen this book before.

Out of 210 people in it only 11 are women.

Well they clearly haven't met my mother.

Or my Nan.

Or Tommy Snotty Norris's mother.

Who is actually hard as ten bears.

Which I found out after I bought him some Kleenex for his fifth birthday present.

I don't know what her problem was. I wrapped them and everything.

No. I don't think the person who wrote that book has ever been to Newport. Or has met anyone who has ever lived here.

Especially not the women.

("JAWS THEME TUNE" plays.)*

SHIT SHIT SHIT.

My phone's ringing. It's my bloody mother. One of the old guys who plays chess in the corner shushes me.

Yes, I know Terry, I'm a librarian. I can't help it, can I? I can't turn the sound off.

But you're shouting "shit."

Yeah fair, play, he's got a point.

I run out into John Square Friar Frost Walk and run-walk down the steps, up past the market and into the underpass with the mosaics that everyone thinks are shit but I love them.

And I don't go left to go home, I go right and I come out onto Newport Bridge just by the castle.

Why am I here? I haven't been here since like, July when I brought Little One down here all dressed up in her knight gear, holding a sword.

We've looked at a book on castles from Nan, before we come, so she's expecting towers and turrets. And she is gutted when she sees the ruins and the rubble and the railings so we can't even get in.

I should have thought that through.

But we still manage to fight a dragon and a massive troll that climbs out from under the bridge.

We win. Obvs.

And as we walk along Newport Bridge I tell her about Houdini,

There was a man once, who did magic tricks and he jumped off this bridge here. With his arms and his hands all tied up. In chains. And he had a sack on his head.

---

* A licence to perform HOW TO BE BRAVE does not include permission to play the Jaws theme tune. For more information, please see the Music Use Note on page v.

Can I have a go?

NO. But she goes to jump and I use my Mum Ninja Surprise Swoop and catch her and whisk her off home under my arm and she bashes my head with her sword all the way.

I don't know why I told her about a mad man jumping into that bogfest but that was mad brave wasn't it. Death defying. YEAH. And I see that there is a mud slide spewing out of one of the castle windows straight into the river. Before I know it I scale the castle railings. I don't know what I am doing but my body vaults, no, not vaults, heaves, itself over. A bit of wall collapses under me. It's stood here for 900 fucking years this stone and the minute I stand on it, it falls a-fucking-part. And then I'm right there at the castle window. And I launch myself down the mud slide and as I go down into the gloopy mud, I give Newport and the whole world the full-on Vs, and I shout like I used to going down the slide at the swimming pool.

BOOOOOLLLLLLLOOOOOOOOCCCCCCCCKKKKKKSSSSS.

—

I'm in Newport Leisure Centre. I'm eleven. And I'm stood on the steps near the top of the slide, in the queue.

Iceland, Iceland. ICELAND! I haven't seen you here before, says Wesley Jacobs, who lives up the road and is a couple of years above me in school.

Oh and by the way, in school everyone called me Iceland. After the supermarket, not the country.

It's my first time.

So you haven't heard?

Heard what?

What they does to the slide?

Who?

Them.

Wesley's pointing at no one in particular but I can see Gemma Tanglethwaite, bane of my life throughout school, prancing like a shire horse in her Naff Naff fucking swimsuit, stuffing her enormous crispy permed hair into a swimming cap. And she just stares at me. And then smiles. THAT smile. The week before she pushed me off the end of the stage in choir practice. The week before that she stole my lunch box and threw in onto the school roof, straight into a puddle. And the day before that she punched me in the throat in Netball. I don't smile back.

Oh right, no I haven't heard Wesley.

There's this test ri'. To get in the gang.

What gang?

THE gang.

Right, and what's the test?

One of them goes down the slide first and puts a razorblade in the cracks. So you'd better watch out for the sharp.

That doesn't make any sense at all, Wesley. Why would anyone put razor blades in a slide and anyway you're moving too quick to actually stop and fit one in the crack and/

Thomson. THOMSON.

Wesley is now shouting to someone further down the steps.

Iceland here doesn't believe me about the razorblades. Show her your leg.

Who is that?

He is one of the gang.

And the other boy, Thomson, shows his leg and he's got this massive scar all down it and then Wesley shouts, *YOUR TURN ICELAND.*

And I'm freaking out. Because of the sharp and the shine on me now as all these eyes stare at me. I don't want a scar like Thomson, no I don't, but I also can't let them see me throw up from the top of the slide. So even though I'm shaking and sick and scared I take a massive run up and jump in the slide head first. And as I cannonball out the bottom I stick my two fingers up at Wesley and Thomson.

Boooollllloooooocckkkkks!

(*Beat.*)

And I'm back in the mud. And there's this shouting and Wesley fucking Jacobs is shouting at me as he clambers over the railings.

ICELAND. ICELAND. ICCCCCEEEEELLLLLLLAAAA NNNNNNDDDDD.

MY NAME IS KATIE, WESLEY. FOR FUCK'S SAKE I AM THIRTY-FIVE. STOP CALLING ME ICELAND.

Then he's next to me trying to get me out of the bog gloop.

What is this mud actually made of? Mid Wales has the River Wye. We have the River What.

ICELAND, WHAT THE FUCK ARE YOU TALKING ABOUT? WHAT ARE YOU DOING IN THERE?

I AM A HOUDINESS.

A fuckin' wha'? And he's pulling me, really hard.

He's got a beard.

(*Escape from mud.*)

And I've lost a dap. And my leg is killing. And I am covered in mud. All I have on me is the packet of wet wipes. I don't think they're going to cut it.

I'm going to have to call my Mother to come pick me up. Only I can't press the buttons on my phone cos my hands are all muddy and cold.

And Wesley says, *Come with me, Iceland.*

(*Beat.*)

Turns out, he owns that new posh café-cocktail-bar, just by the river.

Wesley turns on the lights, takes an upturned chair off a table, sits me down and starts to make me a cup of tea.

What the fuck were you doing in there, Iceland?

The beard suits you.

Yeah, my Missus likes a beard. My daughter doesn't. She says it makes me look like a bad guy.

You got a kid, Wesley.

Three. They're all fucking mental. They take after me, ri'. You got any?

I don't say a word.

I pick up a fork off the table and hold it against his leg and I start to push it in—

OI. THAT'S SHARP.

IS IT? I didn't think you minded a bit of sharp.

Fuck's sake Iceland. What are you doing? Put the fork down. I'll do you some chips.

I don't want any fucking chips.

What about with some cheese on?

I push the fork in even harder.

GET OFF ICELAND. GET OFF.

He's grabbing the fork off me but I won't let go.

You've always been a knobhead, Wesley!

I've just pulled you out the bloody river!

You should shave that beard Wesley. You like a razor blade, don't you?

What the fuck you on about!?

Thomson and the slide, Wesley. Newport Leisure Centre.

Michael Thomson?

Yeah. Him. And his razor blade scarred leg.

He got his scar because his little sister pushed him off his skateboard into some barbed wire because he was being a dick to her. That poor bugger was flattened every day at school so we made up that story about his leg so people would lay off. Sometimes you just got to pretend, don't you? Show you're fucking harder than you are. Pretend. 'Til you are, like. Do something enough and you, like, are it. Right?

Fuck's sake, Wesley.

And I get out of there. I should be somewhere else. I've got wet wipes stuck to the mud all over me. There's blood on my jeans and someone crosses the road to avoid me. I've only got one shoe on. I step on dog poo. Fuck's sake. I need a bike.

And then there it is. The BMX I always wanted as a kid but my parents could never afford. Propped up against some railings. It's another gift from the universe. It must be in the stars.

And it is red and shiny and fast and lush. And I love it. So I just get on it.

And I speed all the way to Belle Vue Park.

It is our favourite park. Because, you know, it is actually the best park in the world. It is massive and beautiful with the flowers and you can get coffee. There are climbing frames and it's steep and like steeped in history, the Chartists started their walk there. And there are giant trees you can climb up and logs you can crawl through and it is grand and lush and it is full of adventures and stories. And THAT view. If you stand in the middle of the park you can see all of everywhere and best of all, you can see the Transporter Bridge, like a beacon.

One day me and Little One go there and walk and chase leaves and fight wasps and Deatheaters. And then we see someone on a bike. Race down the hill, full pelt and then they do an epic skid.

THAT IS THE BRAVEST THING I HAVE ACTUALLY EVER SEEN. I HAVE NEVER SEEN ANYTHING LIKE THAT BEFORE.

Little One cheers and runs up the hill, to copy what she has just seen on her imaginary bike.

Only as she goes up the hill she falls.

But it was a funny fall.

I have never seen anything like that before.

She usually laughs when she's falls down. But she doesn't laugh.

She doesn't get up.

She doesn't move.

And I run to her and I pick her up and her lips are, her lips are all like, well they're blue.

After that, after that day, the next day, she says, *Mummy I want to know what it feels like to come down the hill like that.*

And as I'm circling Belle Vue Park I start getting chased by this shouty dog.

It's really little but it's teeth are huge.

Little One yells at shouty dogs and then they run away.

But I can't do it.

Nothing comes out.

The owner is all, *She won't hurt you. She won't. She just doesn't like bikes. Or people.*

I do zig zags but it's still after me .

I get off the bike and run but it's still after me.

The owner is going crazy now, *Stephanie, Stephanie* – the dog's called Stephanie – *STEPHANIE!*

I get up on a climbing frame and there's kids crying and mothers are throwing rice cakes and water bottles at Stephanie because she's just going for everyone now.

And then some little, brilliant girl rugby tackles the dog and gets it in a headlock, so the owner can finally get her lead back on.

I go back to get the bike.

(Shift.)

I am by St Woolos Cathedral, at the top of Dewsland Park Road.

Little One and me, we call it the Iggly Wiggly way, we always have.

A police car pulls up next to me. And out gets Gemma Tanglethwaite. She still looks like a bastard only worse, because she is now in a police uniform. And she still has massive crispy hair. And she is smiling THAT smile.

Alri' Iceland.

Fuck. I do not need her today.

Alri' Gem?

What are you doing?

What are you doing? I didn't know you were a policeman. Woman. Policewomanman. I mean she is fucking enormous.

I'm a sergeant actually.

Course you are. Course she's found a way to turn bullying into a job.

What are you doing? On that bike?

She starts to get nearer and starts to look at me and the bike, with that glare she has and I say, *I've got an important day today Gemma. I've got to go* and I put my feet on the peddles and push off.

Hang on a minute, she says and tries to get in my way but I manage to swerve her only then I am heading down the Iggly Wiggly Way.

And I hear her footsteps and she's following me so I go quicker and she's running now and I am going down this fucking steep hill and she is getting smaller because I get faster because it's so like iggly and wiggly and steep and I try and slow down but the brakes don't work and I haven't ridden a bike in so long, I don't know what to do. I don't know what the best thing to do is. Pretend until you are doing it, I think. And so I pretend. I'm Geraint Thomas, winning the Tour de Newport. I take the turns and I go, hell bent, helter-skelter all the way down with my hair blowing in the wind. I lift my feet off the pedals and I hold them out. I can fly down hills. Hold on. Just hold on. I shout, *THIS IS HOW IT FEELS LITTLE ONE*, and I get to the bottom. Then I do a wheelie.

I go to get back up onto the pavement from the road, fall up the curb and smash my arm.

(Beat.)

I am in John Frost Square. I am ten years old.

And I'm in this dance troop right?

And there's a show we're doing.

It's epic.

It's to celebrate us getting the clock.

And when I say clock, what I mean is, THE. CLOCK.

"In the Nick of Time" it's actually called but we all just call it THE CLOCK.

And it's been moved from The National Garden Festival for Wales in Ebbw Vale to right in the middle of the square.

This thing is thirty foot tall. And it's made of steel. And it has two massive legs. The actual clock face bit is tiny in comparison to the rest of it. And it opens on the hour, like actually cracks open on purpose, and all these monsters and devils emerge into the air. Like kicking out time in TJs nightclub.

And we are all crammed in, under this clock mountain monster and we have moves and a place to stand and we have direction.

I have a green leotard with, like dragon scales, and diamantés and sequins and I HAVE WINGS.

All of us, little balls of fire and highly flammable hairspray.

The crowds are massive. I mean there are like twenty people but there are photographers and to me that's huge. And there's big girls too, with massive amazing hair and attitude. Shimmying their way into the spotlight.

And the music starts.

The Power by Snap.

I have rehearsed and practised and slept in my costume so I could get used to the itch. I even save up and get a green luminous headband from Fussel Sports.

I know it all.

Every last bit.

I have even studied Gemma Tanglethwaite's facial expressions all the way through Dance Club. Because she is the best, of course. I even have her smile down.

And on the line, *IN THIS THING CALLED RAP*, which is pretty early on mind, I freeze.

Like totally.

Can't move.

Not a muscle.

The girls next to me are all glimmering, glistening and are absolutely having it.

The running man bit and everything.

But my head has fallen out with my arms and legs, and they aren't talking to each other and now the girls are getting furious.

What are you doing? They sneer through their dazzling teeth.

And I just stand there.

Until my Nan comes and takes my hand and leads me to The Wimpy for a sugary pop.

She doesn't say a word.

She doesn't have to.

So we just sit there.

My nickname from then on was Iceland because I froze.

I would still be there now if Nan hadn't grabbed my hand.

And I can feel a hand holding mine now.

But it's Derek. And he is trying to get me up off the floor.

Oh love, you hurt? he says.

My arm's a bit fucked, Derek.

I never swear with Derek.

Let me call your Mum.

And I don't try to stop him.

Thinking about it now, part of me was just relieved I think.

She's on her way. That chain looks a bit wobbly. Let me take a look. Looks like it might come off. And he kneels down and starts trying to sort it.

It's fine Derek, can I have the bike back?

Hang on, oh, here we are.

I can do it.

Just get this bit here and then that bit there.

I've got to go Derek.

Just wait for your Mum now. She was only down the road. She said she was looking for you in the car. She told me she can't come dancing today. Today's the day isn't it?

Give me the bike back, Derek.

It'll be alright, he says, still trying to mend the chain, with his kind hands and his lovely smile. *Sometimes things just need fixing and that's all about it.*

YOU'RE JUST MAKING IT WORSE, and I snatch the bike off him and start cycling off.

Beep Beep Beeeeeeeeeeeeeeeeppppppppppppppppp.

Mum's car is heading up the road. You can't miss Mum's car. It's a bright yellow Fiat Punto.

I cross over the road and go the other way.

Only Mum does a u-turn and pulls up next to me.

WHAT ARE YOU DOING KATIE?

I do a skid, turn the bike round and race off down Mendalgief Road but Mum has found me. So I start to head offroad. There's pigeons going flying and people swearing at me and I am pegging it along the Corpa Road, swerving into factory car parks and down side roads but Mum is on a mission. She beeps and shouts and I go into the Ruby Loftus Estate. Only I go down a dead end. I have to come back on myself and there is the yellow car in all its glory. And she's blocked the road. So I go up a grass verge and mum stalls, because that car is shit. I have my head down so I don't see what direction I'm going in. I go fucking hell for leather. I look up and I've lost Mum, I HAVE LOST MUM. And I mean to go left to go into town but the handlebars go right and I just cycle for about twenty minutes. Just to be sure, just to be sure that I'm on my own. And then I realise I'm totally fucking lost.

And I am in Llanwern.

What the fuck am I doing in Llanwern?

I haven't been down here for years.

Not since it was all the steel works.

And now it's this lovely housing estate, with ponds and ducks.

And then I see it.

In the middle of a roundabout.

The fucking clock.

Why have they moved it here?

It doesn't even work anymore.

It's just stuck.

And I hate it.

I hate that fucking clock.

I cycle over to the roundabout and I start hitting it. First with my fists, then with my shitty shoe but that's not enough so I start crashing the bike into the clock. But it just stands there. Not moving. Cos, you know, it's made of steel. So I ride the bike into the clock.

OI. Mental. Leave that fucking clock alone.

FUCK OFF!

People love this bastard thing.

Beep, Beep, Beeeeepppppppppppppppppppppppppppppp pppp.

FUCK OFF AND DIE!

And right there is Little One. Right. There. Her face just, just drops. The yellow car has stopped in the middle of the road, hazard lights flashing. Little One is cwtched up in the back in her pyjamas and dressing gown and she starts to cry. Big splashy tears.

And Mum, who is marching towards me, just turns around and gets back in and starts the engine.

Only it's stalled.

And I run to Little One's door. But it's locked.

And I try the passenger door. But it's locked.

LET ME IN. LET ME IN, LET ME IN, LET ME IN. OPEN THIS DOOR MOTHER.

I AM NOT LETTING YOU IN THIS CAR KATIE. Look at the absolute state of you. This can't keep happening. What kind of a thing is this to show her? This is not what she needs, is it?

I don't know, let's ask her. And I lean in through the open window. *What do you want, Little One?*

I wish… I wish you weren't my Mummy.

And she looks the other way.

And the engine starts up.

There. You see? I am taking her. I am taking her away from you, right now, and they're gone.

No. No. NO.

And I run to get on the bike because all I want to do is chase after them. Catch up with them, hang onto the bumper and climb through the window, but after I've thrown the bike into a massive steel leg, the chain has now come fully off.

Sometimes things just need fixing. And that's all about it. Fucking Derek.

I look up and I am right under that bastard frozen clock.

But for once, I'm not frozen.

(The music starts. Katie starts the dance and it's like the dance of a ten year old, who's actually a thirty-five year old and who's a bit unfit and is struggling to remember the same dance from twenty-four years ago.)

(Katie does the routine. It is an absolute release of fight and fear and she is punching the air with all her might.)

I HAVE IMMENSE MUSCLE MEMORY.

(Dance ends.)

(Katie bows.)

Just keep moving.

But I can't go yet, not before I go and tell Nan what I've done. That I have actually done it. All the way through. In public.

Sometimes things just need fixing. And that's all about it. Thanks Derek.

I reattach the chain. And I get back on the bike.

I steam through Lliswery, over the new bridge, up through Pill.

I'm totally out of puff now though. Totally running out of steam. So I slow down and weave in and out of the streets and the people. And I have to rest. So I perch against a wall. Dancing is so much easier when you're eleven.

Then someone comes towards me. A man, in like his sixties, with a blue hat on and some very fetching leisure wear. And he's holding a can of Special VAT.

Love. Oh. Love. Do you want a buy a pigeon?

And I see he is carrying a blue plastic bag with a pigeon in it. Not a dead one. A real life one that is flapping its wings like mad trying to get out of there. But he holds this bag so tight it can't get out.

And a lady pulls her child away but Pigeon Man comes nearer. And he comes and pats my back. He even offers me some of his Special VAT. I don't take any.

You look like you need someone to talk to. I'll do you a discount on my pigeon. He's a very good listener.

I give him my £5.34 and I cycle up by the river and the bike starts to feel a bit knackered now, the pigeon makes funny noises as I peddle, but I carry on, back to the castle. And I stop and let the pigeon out of the bag and it flies away, like furious, into town. And I follow it.

And it's up high and I watch as it swoops around all these buildings. From where I am they look like empty shells, so many of them, empty, closed down. Watching this manky bird, I can see they used to be something. I can see all their former glory. I used to be something. It used to be really clear what Newport was. And it used to be really clear what I was. It's not so clear now. But it's still there.

(Beat.)

I go up Barrack Hill to get to Nan's.

The chain clicks.

The pedals lock.

And the bike breaks right outside the Barracks and I smash my nose on the handle bars.

(Beat.)

I'm in Nan's Prefab. I'm twenty-three.

The Prefab is still tin. They haven't done them up yet. And Nan loves living here. And I love visiting. I'm here all the time.

Nan's is Number Five. Just down from the one that exploded.

The tele is on and we just watch. And chat and wait for This Morning to come on.

Only it doesn't come on. The News does instead.

There's been bombs in London. And it's just horror. The world has changed.

Nan's gone into the kitchen to make me some stupidly strong squash.

When she comes back she just says, *Oh no.*

And we watch and cry and I hold her hand.

What do we do Nan? I say.

There's always been bad, she says.

But not like this. This is new. Worse.

And she looks at me. *I've seen it before. We had bombs going off here. I remember standing up on Ridgeway and seeing Newport on fire.*

What did you do?

We helped didn't we. Women all over Newport were working, making ammunitions, mending people.

Is that why you're so good at fixing stuff, Nan?

And someone on the news, who had survived, was talking about the noise. That when the explosion occurred, the sound was both deafening and silent at once.

What did it sound like? The war?

Like the end of the world. There was an anti-aircraft gun up at the barracks. And shots used to ring out in the middle of the night, as they tried to shoot down the planes that were dropping bombs on us. They fell all over us – the docks, Rogerstone, the Gaer, Stow Park, the river/

*How did you live with that? With that terror. I don't think
I could.*

*You are forgetting what we are made of my girl. We are
from Newport. People like to turn their noses up at us but
we are made of strong stuff. We have steel in us, and fight
and loyalty. We get knocked down but we get up again. Over
and over. We rebuild. We rise. We have grit. Something bad
is always around the corner. Waiting. We can't let the bad
win. We stand up to the fear. We march on. We mend. We are
made of stuff stronger then we'll ever understand. The iron
in our blood and the carbon in our bones have come from
the stars themselves. We are made of particles of exploded
supernovas and star dust. I've got this book, look...*

And Nan gets this science book out and we read and look.
And she says,

*How can you not feel brave when you know that? You just
need to remember that even in the dark that light and power
is in us all.*

She always knows what to say at the right moment, Nan.

I come back round on top of this hill and I know that she
is who I need to speak to most on today of all days.

So I pick up the bits of the totally broken bike and march
on up to Ridgeway.

And I go round the corner to get to Number Five.

I start to shake.

And I go and stand at the front door.

But my legs are shaking so much that I have to sit down.

It doesn't help. I'm so dizzy now that I have to lie down.

I lie on the doorstep.

And I do the secret knock on Nan's door.

There is no answer.

And so I do it again louder.

Still nothing.

I bang and bang and bang.

And the door opens. And just for a second, just for a milli-of-a-second, I think it's her but there's this strange old lady staring down at me as I lie on her door step.

(Beat.)

And the old lady who isn't my nan closes the door on me.

And I stay exactly where I am. Because I can't do anything else. Nothing will work.

And then I hear the car pull up.

MUM? Little One?

And I see this pair of shiny black boots approaching me.

Jesus Iceland and Gemma Tanglethwaite is stood looking down on me, like she always does.

I'm lying on the step of Number Five thinking, *here we go, here we fucking go.*

Get up Katie, she orders. *You can't stay here.*

No. I can't stay here. I can't. I need to get away. I've got to get away. And I get on my hands and knees and I start crawling.

ICELAND!

And I jump up. I can see Gemma's police car and I am filled with rage. I take a flying leap at the passenger door and am kicking it with all my might. And I try to rip the wing mirror off and I'm punching the windows and Gemma Tanglefuck puts me in some kind of arm lock, cuffs me and shoves me in the back of the car.

She gets in the front, takes her hat off.

GO ON. GO ON THEN. TAKE ME IN.

What's that in your hair, Katie? Is that river mud? Because there was a report earlier of a trespassing incident at Newport Castle. There's videos on YouTube.

I don't say a word.

And is that your broken bike out there? The children's one? Because there was a kid's BMX reported stolen earlier. And that one does look a bit small for you.

YES. Yes I fucking stole it. I stole a child's bike from some railings on Stow Hill.

And you're also intimidating old ladies on their doorsteps. That old dear has called us, terrified.

And she is staring THAT stare at me in the rear view mirror.

Were you in Llanwern today? Because there was a traffic accident on the roundabout caused by and I quote – and she gets her fucking notebook out – *a mad woman covered in mud and blood dancing under the clock and repeatedly crashing a BMX into it. What were you doing vandalising a well-loved monument? What the hell is going on, Iceland?*

I am not answering her. I'm not.

What if I just took you home?

NO. FUCKING NO. NO WAY.

Has something happened at home, Katie? Is that why you want me to take you in? Are you scared of someone at home?

And then it just comes out, *Yes I'm fucking scared, I am scared of my fucking little girl, I am scared... Fuck Gemma. She's got an operation. Little One. She's going in now. There's a valve in her heart. FUCK YOU FUCKTHWAIT!*

And something in her eyes changes.

Gemma starts the ignition. She puts the lights on and the sirens blare and we are going to the police station. She drives down Ridgeway, down Risca Road and handbrake turns down the Iggly Wiggly Way. At the bottom of the hill, on the junction, I can see the police station. But we go the other way. And she skids right outside the doors of the Royal Gwent Hospital and slams on the breaks.

Gemma jumps out the car, puts on her hat, opens my door and I try to run away from her but she pulls me back. Man she is strong.

And she keeps one cuff on me and puts the other one on herself. She has bastard handcuffed me to her. *We are in this together*, she says. And I have no choice. She drags me with her into the hospital to the reception, pulls me up the stairs and leads me down the labyrinth of corridors. The two of us cuffed together crash through the doors to Little One's ward. But she's gone.

She's gone down.

But Gemma won't give up and she flashes her badge a few times, and her hair, and we are near the operating room then. And there she is. In her bed. And there's an Anaesthetist and a Nurse and there's beeps and wires.

Where have you been? Little One's face is fierce with rage. And my eyes are leaking and I can't find any words.

She's been helping me. Your Mum came here in a police car, with the lights and siren going and wearing handcuffs.

You brought me a police woman!

Gemma high fives Little One and I see she is wearing this amazing patchwork quilt of all her superhero costumes; Wonder Woman, Ironman, Spiderman, Elsa cape bits, all fixed together with sticky tape.

I couldn't decide which one to wear so I cut them all up so I could put them all on.

And my heart swells with pride. But nothing comes out. I can't say anything.

But I couldn't find my tiara before we had to leave.

Gemma removes the cuffs and takes off her police hat. *Will this do?* and she puts it on Little One's head. And Little One beams. And sunshine fills the room.

NOW I AM SUPER BRAVE. Just like you, a police woman.

Just like your Mum. Your Mum was the bravest girl in school. Did you know that? Some people were really horrible to her. But she was always kind. She was honest, she was always herself. She knew what she had inside was enough and that's magic. How brave is that?

It's super brave! What else is brave? Little One asks.

Well, brave is showing up when you are really scared. And dancing in public. Katie, what do you think?

I look at Little One's expectant face. *Riding your bike down a really steep hill, with no breaks.*

And I remember it all now.

Diving into the deep end at Risca Leisure Centre. Being on live tele, with braces, and a terrible fringe when I won a Blue Peter Badge for making a spaghetti bridge. Standing next to the bully at school and thinking she's not a total dickhead.

And Little One leans into Gemma, *Did you know my Mummy is really fast. One day, when I was really poorly, in the park, she carried me all the way to the hospital, running so so so fast. Like she had wings. My Mummy. I've got my wings on too.*

And she leans forward and her Rainbow Wings explode open.

And I wrap my arms around her and give her everything I have.

And I turn around and Gemma is leaving without her hat.

The Anaesthetist needs to do her thing.

I got to go to the fixing place now, Mummy.

I know, Little One.

I'm going to get really sleepy in a minute. Can you tell me a bedtime story?

Yes. Of course. What should it be about?

About you!

OK. So let me tell you about Mummy, the mad woman who jumped into a bogfest.

And her eyes pop open.

And then the countdown starts.

Ten

This is a story

Nine

about how much

Eight

Mummy

Seven

loves you.

But she'd already gone. She was out. And they wheel her away. And the doors slam shut.

And it sounds like the end of the world.

(Beat.)

They show me into the waiting room.

There's my Mum. And I'm terrified she is going to scream or yell, or worse, not say anything at all. And I look at her. But she doesn't look back. So with all my might I walk towards her. And sit right next to her. And she still won't look at me. She doesn't move. And so I grab Mum's face and I tell her. Tell her what I haven't told anyone.

I'm so scared. I am so scared I am going to lose Little One. I ran away because it's my fault. I couldn't face it. I couldn't face her. Because I made her broken. I carried her but I let her down. I'm a bad mum. I don't work like I should so neither does she. It's my fault , it's my fault, it's my fault.

Mum puts her hands on my face. And she says,

You weren't running away. You were just trying to find your brave. And you're here now. And I'm so proud of you.

And I grab her. Like I did when I was little. And I can't let go.

And the tears come then. And they won't stop. But then I get the panic.

I've got all this stuff I want to tell her, I tried to tell her but I was too late. What if I don't get the chance, what if I don't get the chance to tell her?

Write it all down, Mum says.

What? I say.

Yeah. Like a book. Write her a book.

And she takes out this notebook from her bag and rips some pages out that she's written in and gives the notebook to me.

But I don't know how to write a book.

You read enough of them. What are your favourite books?

The how-to books that Nan gave me.

Why don't we write it like that then. An actual how to.

I wouldn't even know where to start.

With a title.

How to be a terrible mother?

How to be brave.

I miss Nan.

Me too.

And then we just fall silent and write and wait together.

(Beat.)

Hospitals are funny places aren't they?

They are a half-way house.

Souls arriving, leaving. It all just hangs in the air.

And as we wait, I can feel that it's not just us in that room.

I go to the window and look out over Newport and all it holds.

And I can see them all.

All of them who came before.

That stood on that bridge.

Or went under,

Or floated along,

Or who got swept along by its mad tides.

All the cherubs.

All those who made marks on the wall.

All the hidden treasures.

All those that shouted into the wind

All the words spoken,

All the exhales.

And I open the window.

And I breathe it all in.

The steel

The grit

The battle

The ammunition

The shots fired in the sky

The shadows

The light

The fight

The hope

It's all in the air

The particles of it all

The fucking stars

The remnants

The atoms and the bomb parts

It all wraps itself around me

It enfolds me.

And my brain sparks.

And I realise that we are fucking magic.

We ride the storms

We go with the tides

We stick together.

We may be made of bits of broken and medieval sea and
wars and knocked-down buildings and giant hotels and

fallen down castles and we are knackered and a bit rough around the edges. We may be shadows of our former selves but it is still all in us.

We are made like no others.

We are mothers

We are grandmothers

We are daughters

And we are all those that have come before.

We fix, we make, we mend.

We RISE.

We are brave as fuck.

End

VISIT THE SAMUEL FRENCH BOOKSHOP AT THE ROYAL COURT THEATRE

Browse plays and theatre books, get expert advice and enjoy a coffee

Samuel French Bookshop
Royal Court Theatre
Sloane Square
London
SW1W 8AS
020 7565 5024

Shop from thousands of titles on our website

 samuelfrench.co.uk

 samuelfrenchltd

 samuel french uk

Lightning Source UK Ltd.
Milton Keynes UK
UKHW022353230719
346693UK00005B/128/P